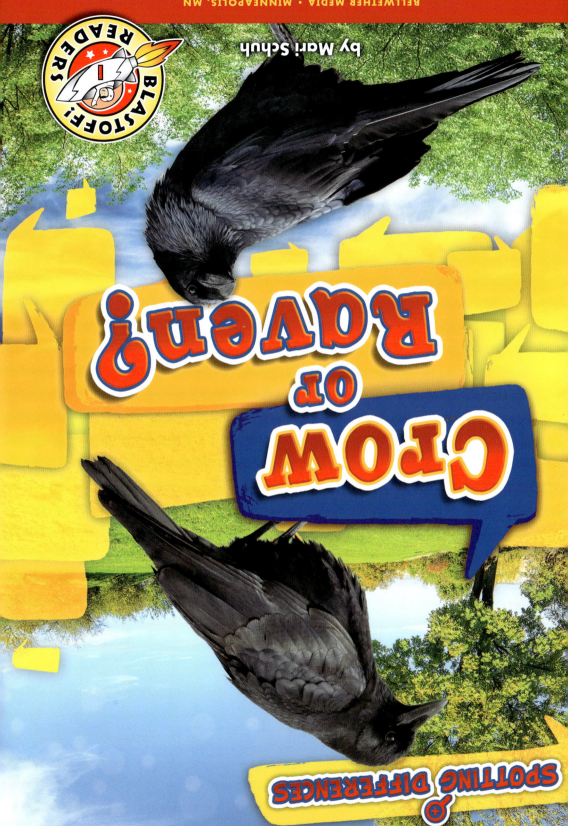

Blastoff! Readers are carefully developed by literacy experts to build reading stamina and move students toward fluency by combining standards-based content with developmentally appropriate text.

Level 1 provides the most support through repetition of high-frequency words, light text, predictable sentence patterns, and strong visual support.

Level 2 offers early readers a bit more challenge through varied sentences, increased text load, and text-supportive special features.

Level 3 advances early-fluent readers toward fluency through increased text load, less reliance on photos, advancing concepts, longer sentences, and more complex special features.

★ **Blastoff! Universe**

Reading Level

Grade **K**

Grades **1–3**

Grade **4**

This edition first published in 2023 by Bellwether Media, Inc.

No part of this publication may be reproduced in whole or in part without written permission of the publisher. For information regarding permission, write to Bellwether Media, Inc., Attention: Permissions Department, 6012 Blue Circle Drive, Minnetonka, MN 55343.

Library of Congress Cataloging-in-Publication Data

Names: Schuh, Mari C., 1975- author.
Title: Crow or raven? / by Mari Schuh.
Description: Minneapolis, MN : Bellwether Media, Inc., 2023. | Series: Blastoff! readers: spotting differences | Includes bibliographical references and index. | Audience: Ages 5-8 | Audience: Grades K-1 |
Summary: "Developed by literacy experts for students in kindergarten through grade three, this book introduces crows and ravens to young readers through leveled text and related photos"-- Provided by publisher.
Identifiers: LCCN 2021062913 (print) | LCCN 2021062914 (ebook) | ISBN 9781644876961 (library binding) | ISBN 9781648347429 (ebook)
Subjects: LCSH: Crows--Juvenile literature. | Ravens--Juvenile literature.
Classification: LCC QL696.P2367 S38 2023 (print) | LCC QL696.P2367 ebook) | DDC 598.8/64--dc23/eng/20220104
LC record available at https://lccn.loc.gov/2021062913
LC ebook record available at https://lccn.loc.gov/2021062914

Text copyright © 2023 by Bellwether Media, Inc. BLASTOFF! READERS and associated logos are trademarks and/or registered trademarks of Bellwether Media, Inc.

Editor: Elizabeth Neuenfeldt   Designer: Laura Sowers

Printed in the United States of America, North Mankato, MN.

Table of Contents

Crows and Ravens   4
Different Looks   8
Different Lives   16
Side by Side   20
Glossary   22
To Learn More   23
Index   24

Crows and Ravens

Crows and ravens are black **songbirds**. They look a lot alike!

Ravens and crows live in many **habitats**. Can you tell these songbirds apart?

crow

Different Looks

Both birds have **beaks**.
Raven beaks are bigger.

8

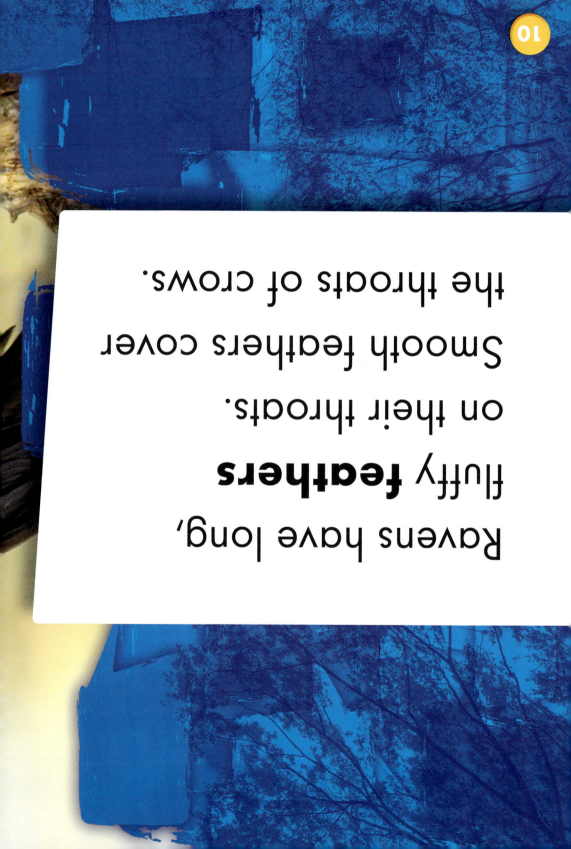

Ravens have long, fluffy **feathers** on their throats. Smooth feathers cover the throats of crows.

10

↑
feathers

12

Both birds are big.
But ravens are bigger than crows.

13

14

Crows have tails shaped like fans. Ravens have tails shaped like **wedges**.

wedge

Different Lives

Crows flap their wings more as they fly. Ravens often **soar**. Ravens also fly upside down!

Ravens often travel alone or in pairs. Crows often travel in groups. Which are these?

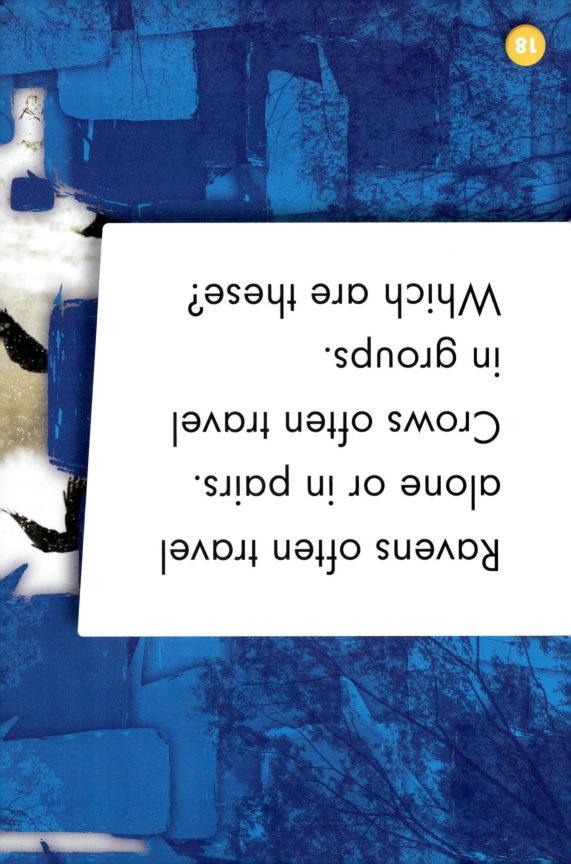

Crow Differences

flap wings often

often travel in groups

Side by Side

- tail shaped like a fan
- smaller body
- smooth feathers on throat
- smaller beak

Glossary

habitats
the places where animals live

feathers
light, soft coverings on the bodies of birds

beaks
the hard front parts of the mouths of birds

wedges
things that are shaped like triangles

songbirds
birds that make musical sounds

soar
to fly or glide high in the air without flapping wings

To Learn More

AT THE LIBRARY

Barnes, Rachael. *Crows*. Minneapolis, Minn.: Bellwether Media, 2023.

Lajiness, Katie. *Ravens: Problem Solvers*. Minneapolis, Minn.: Abdo Publishing, 2019.

Lynch, Seth. *Birds Close Up*. New York, N.Y.: Gareth Stevens Publishing, 2023.

ON THE WEB

FACTSURFER

Factsurfer.com gives you a safe, fun way to find more information.

1. Go to www.factsurfer.com.
2. Enter "crow or raven" into the search box and click Q.
3. Select your book cover to see a list of related content.

Index

beaks, 8, 9

fans, 14

feathers, 10, 11

fly, 16

groups, 18

habitats, 6

pairs, 18

size, 8, 12

soar, 16

songbirds, 4, 6

tails, 14

travel, 18

wedges, 14, 15

wings, 16

The images in this book are reproduced through the courtesy of: David Spates, front cover (crow); Marcin Krzyzak, front cover (top background); Tom Meaker, front cover (raven); sommai damrongpanich, front cover (bottom background); Piotr Krzeslak, pp. 4-5; del13, pp. 6-7; Jukka Jantunen, pp. 8-9; Krasula, p. 9; WildMedia, pp. 10-11; Randy Bjorklund, pp. 11, 20 (crow); fernando sanchez, pp. 12-13; Sundry Photography, p. 13; Miroslav Hlavko, pp. 14-15; Paul Reeves Photography, p. 15; Nature Picture Library/ Alamy, pp. 16-17; Fotokostic, pp. 18-19; rck_953, p. 20 (travel in groups); Tanor, p. 20 (flap wings often); Rosa Jay, p. 21 (raven); Ryzhkov Sergy, p. 21 (travel alone); ASakoulis, p. 21 (often soar); fernando sanchez, p. 22 (beaks); BGSmith, p. 22 (feathers); ilkah, p. 22 (habitats); rck_953, p. 22 (soar); Hergon, p. 22 (songbirds); Rafal Szozda, p. 22 (wedges).